Christianity
FOR BEGINNERS

MIKE MAZZALONGO

THE "FOR BEGINNERS" SERIES

The "For Beginners" series of video classes and books provide a non-technical and easy to understand presentation of Bible books and topics that are rich in information and application for the beginner as well as the mature Bible student.

For more information about these books, visit:
bibletalk.tv/for-beginners

BibleTalk Books
14998 E. Reno
Choctaw, Oklahoma 73020

TABLE OF CONTENTS

A NOTE FOR READERS

This book is designed for those who are new to the Christian religion and for those who want a refresher course on the basic ideas upon which Christianity is based. There are seven chapters in the book:

1. **Belief in God** – The basic reason why we believe in God, or a Supreme Being.

2. **The Christian Religion** – A study of the major religions in the world and how Christianity compares to these.

3. **The Bible** – A brief look at how the Bible was written, how it came to us in its present form, and why we believe that it is revelation or inspired by God.

4. **Jesus Christ** – This chapter will focus on the central figure in Christianity, Jesus Christ.

5. **Salvation** – In this chapter we will review the main idea of the Christian religion which is its solution to mankind's greatest problem - sin.

6. **The Church** – We will examine what Jesus and the Apostles say about the church and how the Bible describes it.

7. **The Christian Lifestyle** – Our final chapter will describe what is the style and purpose of Christian life.

Of course, Jesus Christ, the Bible, and the church, as well as all of these other subjects can take many years of study to fully understand and appreciate. However, this book is given as a brief introduction, a summary of the Christian religion and its beliefs in order to help students begin their journey of faith and the blessings that come as a result.

1.

BELIEF IN GOD

When it comes to any religion, including Christianity, the beginning point is a belief in God. Most people believe what their parents and grandparents believed about God. When we examine the question a little more objectively however, we find out that there are many ideas about God.

- Some believe there is no God and that this life is all there is.

- Some believe that there are many gods that exist in nature and beyond nature.

- Still others believe that there is only one God and that He is supreme over all things and people.

Most religions in the world are based on the belief that there is one or many gods and we'll examine these religions more closely in our next chapter. In this chapter we want to examine what Christianity believes about God and why.

What Christianity Believes About God

Christians arrive at their conclusions about God based on three sources.

#1 - Human Reasoning

Human beings have asked themselves about the existence of God throughout history. The various thoughts and theories about the existence of God have produced several key arguments that support, from human reason and observation, the idea that there is a God. Here are a few of these arguments.

The First Cause Argument

If every effect has a cause, what or who caused the world to come into existence? Scientists can only say that they believe that the universe and all life in the universe are the result of a "Big Bang" or cosmic explosion millions even billions of years ago. They cannot, however, explain what or who caused this explosion. The "first cause" argument says that a being greater and more complex than the universe (God) caused this big bang and set the creation of the world into motion.

The Complexity Argument

This reasoning says that only a complex mind could have conceived and created a complex world. Since complex, living, animate beings cannot naturally come from simple, non-living, inanimate matter (for example a bird cannot evolve from a stone) then the world of matter and animated beings must have been conceived and created by a being more complex than His creation (God). For example, a person creates a computer not the other way around.

The Moral/Spiritual Argument

The desire to do right, or be good does not exist in simple matter. Even in higher life forms like monkeys for example the need to search for God, to reach up and worship a higher being is not present. Where does this moral/spiritual element come from? It does not evolve from matter or lower animals. We reason that it comes from above humanity - God.

These are some, but not all of the arguments of purely human thought and conclusions about the existence of God.

Christianity's belief in God includes this human reasoning but has two other sources of information to base its belief in a Supreme Being.

#2 - The Bible

We will study about the history and content of the Bible in our 3rd chapter, but for now let us just say that the Bible contains information about who God is and not just that He exists. Christianity's concept of the personality of God is based on the revealing (or revelation) of His character and actions in the Bible.

Someone could say, "How do we know that the Bible's information is reliable?" I will answer this question and more in our 3rd chapter. For now let us just look at some of the things the Bible actually says about God.

He created the world and human life.

Genesis 1:1;27 "In the beginning God created the heavens and the earth." "So God created human beings in His own image, in the image of God He created them. Male and female He created them." The Bible does not explain how God did this, although scientists throughout the ages continue to discover piece-by-piece the way the world is put together. The Bible simply tells us that an all-powerful, intelligent, moral being (which we refer to as God) created the physical universe by an act of His will.

God loves His creation, especially humans.

> "For God loved the world so much that He gave his one and only Son…"
> - John 3:16a

God will judge the world.

> "And remember that the heavenly Father has no favorites. He will judge or reward you according to what you do."
> - I Peter 1:17

The point I want to make here is that by human reasoning we can come to know that there is a Supreme Being, a God who is greater than we are and greater than the world. However, human reason cannot reveal to us God's character, His will and purpose, or communication with us as human beings. Christians believe that this personal and particular information about God is only revealed in the Bible (and in chapter 3 I will explain why we believe this information is accurate). So we have human reasoning and the Bible as sources of information about God's existence, character, and will. There is one other source of information about God, however, that is surer and clearer than these two. This source is not based on human thought or a book. This information comes from a person.

#3 - Jesus Christ

There have been countless books written about Jesus Christ but the basic information about Him comes from the Bible. Other writers throughout history have written about Him, about His life and teachings, about the meaning and practice of what He said, however, only the Bible contains eyewitness accounts of His life, death and resurrection from the dead. Jesus Christ presents the clearest picture of God's character and His will for our lives. The reason for this is that Jesus Christ is God.

In chapter 4 we will look more closely at this claim and why Christians believe this to be true, but for now we will assume that this is true.

The Bible teaches that God, the Supreme Being, creator of the universe, took on a human form and entered the physical world in order to reveal Himself clearly and in a way that human beings could understand and relate to.

That human being's name was Jesus, son of Joseph of Nazareth. We refer to Him as Jesus Christ because the word Christ is a title that means "Anointed One."

And so Jesus' life, teachings, and examples give us the clearest view yet of who God is and what He is like. If we examine Jesus' life we are able to find things out about God that no words in a book or human reasoning can reveal:

1. God has compassion for those who are weak.

Those who followed Jesus and recorded their eyewitness accounts of His life and work repeatedly mention His kindness and compassion to those who were sick, handicapped, had emotional problems or were failures in areas of morality and self-control. He encouraged those who were poor or socially outcast or were different culturally than the mainstream. Jesus demonstrated a part of God's character that could not be shown by creative power alone. Without Jesus I could know that God had the power to create the sun, but through Jesus I learn that God also loves small children.

Jesus' life and teachings are filled with these revelations about who God really is and what He is like. Perhaps the most important insight that we can gain through Jesus is what God wants.

2. God wants people to have eternal life with Him.

Here are Jesus' own words concerning this subject in the gospel of John (one of Jesus' Apostles):

> "For this is the will of My Father, that everyone who beholds the Son and believes in Him will have eternal life, and I Myself will raise him up on the last day."
> - John 6:40

In this passage Jesus reveals several very important things about God that we could not know in any other way except that it be shown to us by Him.

"For this is the will of My Father"

That God (Jesus calls Him my Father because Jesus and God have the same divine nature) has a particular purpose or plan for each of us. Life is not just a bunch of random events that ends in physical death.

"that everyone who beholds the Son and believes in Him"

That God has a requirement of us. God wants people to believe in Him and the way to do that is to believe (accept as true) that He has revealed Himself in Jesus. So we learn that as far as God is concerned, it is important what you believe. He says that belief in Him and belief in Jesus is the same thing.

"will have eternal life"

God's plan is that we have eternal life. Life's greatest questions revolve around death and what, if anything, happens after death. God takes on human form, proves that He is God by doing miracles (extraordinary acts that only God could do) and then says that His plan for mankind is for human beings to live eternally. There is a certain portion of the Bible called the "Good News" or the "Gospel". It is that section in the Bible that describes Jesus, His life, and ministry. The reason it is called the "Good News" is because God has come in human form to announce to the world that there is life after death - no need to be afraid anymore - now that is Good News!

"and I Myself will raise him up on the last day."

Here we have 2 more pieces of information given to us by Jesus, which we could not know in any other way.

That it is Jesus that will give eternal life and not anyone else.

This helps us to focus our attention on one religious leader, Jesus, the only one who promises and demonstrates that He has the power over life and death. We also read in the Bible that Jesus is killed but then resurrects from the dead and His resurrection is witnessed by hundreds of people. The point, of course, is that if He has power over His own death and resurrection as God, then He naturally has power over everyone else's life and death as God.

Finally, this passage shows that there will be an end to time as we know it.

Just as the Bible shows at the very start that God created the world and the beginning of "time." Jesus says that there will be the end of the world and "time." And this is when He will raise to eternal life all those who believed in Him. Now we've only looked at two things that Jesus reveals about God that we could not know in any other way:

1. His compassion for those who are weak.

2. His plan and purpose for mankind.

A careful study of Jesus' life would yield many more revelations about God, but I've given you these two as examples of how Christians come to know and believe in God.

Summary

Let us summarize what we have talked about in this first chapter in our series "Christianity for Beginners." This chapter is entitled "Belief in God." Here are some of the points we covered:

1. We can come to know and believe in God through various methods.

Christians rely on three main ways:

A. Human Reasoning - Human reasoning suggests that it is quite logical to accept that there is a God.

B. Bible Records - The Bible records God's dealings with man from the creation of the world to the formation of the Christian church. It describes God's character and purpose in His interactions with mankind.

C. Jesus Christ - Jesus is the human embodiment of God and through Him the most intimate and revealing aspects of God's nature and will can be known.

2. There are many opinions and beliefs about spirits, gods, divine powers, but **Christians believe that the Bible and witness of Jesus Christ provide the most accurate and reliable information about God and His will.**

This is not to say that there are not elements of truth about God in various philosophies and religions that exist or there are many valuable spiritual insights contained in each major religion throughout history. However, Christians believe that the clearest and most complete revelation of God, His purpose and plan for man's life now and in the future has been revealed once and for all time by the Bible and especially through Jesus Christ. Hopefully, as we complete the next six chapters in this book you also will be more convinced that this is so.

#1 - Belief in God
Discussion Questions

Which of the natural arguments for the existence of God is strongest? Why? Which is the weakest? Why?

Can someone who doesn't believe in God have a moral code? What would it be based on?

Why should the Bible be considered a reliable source of information about the existence of God?

2.
THE
CHRISTIAN RELIGION

In this chapter we are going to look at the Christian religion from a wide view as we compare it to other major religions in the world. This comparison will help us in three ways:

1. **Historical context** - We will be able to see where Christianity fits in the general history of mankind and history of other religions.

2. **Understanding** - By examining Christianity alongside other religions and their main ideas, we will be better able to understand the claims, teachings, and benefits of the Christian religion.

3. **Appreciation** - We often fail to appreciate the value of what we have until we compare it to some other similar thing. The value of the Christian religion becomes more evident when it is compared to the teachings and claims of other world religions.

At the end of this study I hope that you will not only more fully understand Christianity but will also appreciate its incalculable value in your life.

Major Religions of the World

When speaking of the religions of the world many people think that there are literally hundreds or even thousands of groups and beliefs in the world when in fact there are really only about a dozen organized religions if you include what's called "primitive religions."

1. Religion

The dictionary defines "religion" as "...man's expression of his acknowledgement of the Divine..." The Bible writers use the word religion in describing the ceremonies that the Jews did in expressing their faith – (Acts 26:5). When we talk about the religions of the world we are referring to the different ways mankind has developed to express the idea that there is something other than himself (usually higher) here in this world.

Christians believe that Christianity is not a man-made religion but rather given to us by God. However, for the purpose of this book, I will put it alongside other religions in order to see where it fits in historically and theologically. On the other hand, there are many philosophies and movements that come and go throughout history which have impacted society but are not necessarily religions, for example:

- **New Age Movement** - combination of ideas from existing religions and philosophies.

- **Communism** - political and ideological movement.

- **Naturalism** - outgrowth of Atheism, tries to explain world without God.

These and others have had influence on the world but are not considered organized religions.

2. Organized Religions

In order for something to be a religion it needs certain features:

- **History/origins** - all religions can trace their origins to a place or a person.
- **Concept of Deity** - main feature of religion is that it acknowledges the existence of a higher being or power.
- **Concept of mankind** - a key question that most religions try to answer is, "Where did man come from?" and each religion has an explanation of some kind.
- **Salvation** - each religion has its own answer to the problem of the human condition and some offer of a better existence.
- **Worship** - most religions provide their own ceremonies that express their faith. These are done as individuals or collectively.
- **Scriptures** - religions keep records of their founders, teachings, history, worship, etc.
- **Geography** - most religions have certain countries where they begin and flourish and where they exercise their influence.

Not every religion exhibits each one of these features, but most of them have a majority in common. The nature of our study will be to compare the different religions of the world according to these categories.

Primitive Religions

Before we discuss the major world religions however, I think that it would be helpful to talk for a moment about what are called "primitive religions." These do not fit into the pattern of major, organized, world religions but are ideas practiced by many in the ancient world and even in today's society but in very different and disorganized ways. Some features of primitive religions include:

- Strong belief in magic.
- No individual God or gods or powers.
- Practiced in various forms including:
  - **Animism** - objects inhabited by spirits (charms, etc.).
  - **Dynamism** - impersonal forces at work in nature (e.g. sacred burial or hunting places).
  - **Fetishism** - an object into which power is introduced (e.g. voodoo).
  - **Totemism** - association of animal and human characteristics. Practiced by Native American Indians.

These types of primitive religions kept few written records, had little organized theological thought or worship, and mostly focused on nature and man's relationship with his environment. We can trace primitive religions historically:

- From early tribal groups - 4000 BC
- To Egyptian nature and mystery cults - 3200 BC
- Babylonians introduced magic/astrology to the mix - 3000 BC
- The Greeks began with primitive nature religion that evolved through a mythological stage (many gods) to a philosophical stage and end up as a mix with Roman style mythology (the Romans took the Greek gods and gave them Roman names: Zeus=Jupiter).
- The Romans mixed Greek mythology with their own primitive nature religions.
- Eventually the Roman religion was eclipsed by Christianity.

However, you still see traces of ancient Roman primitive religion in the Catholic form of Christianity with its saints, images, candles, and mystical practices.

I mention primitive religions because they are still practiced in many countries today (e.g. voodoo in Haiti and Native American peoples in North America) and many ideas from primitive religions are recirculating today in other forms (New Age Movement - emphasis on the pre-eminence of the environment / Falun Gong in China trying to harness spiritual power through physical means). But primitive religions are not part of the group of major world religions that are practiced by the majority of the populations on earth in the last 2000 years or so.

Major Religions

As I mentioned previously, not counting primitive religions, there are only 11 major organized religions in the world. These are usually listed in geographical terms based on where they began. We will review and summarize each briefly beginning with the least familiar first.

Far Eastern Religions (China, Japan)

1. Taoism (China)

Founded by Lao-Tze (604-517 BC)
Major ideas:

- Man is the highest level. To experience God one had to look within man and nature and find "balance" in life. (e.g. ying/yang)

- Taoists reject all human institutions as counterproductive.

2. Confucianism (China)

Founded by King-Fu-Tze (551-478 BC)
Major ideas:

- No heaven or hell for people.
- The focus was on the proper relationship between people in a society by cultivating basic personal virtues.
- The practice of this "religion" was the cultivation of these virtues (e.g. wisdom, good morals, etc.) based on his teachings.

3. Shinto (Japan)

No founder - evolved from a basic "nature" religion and added concepts from Taoism, Confucianism, Buddhism.

Main ideas:

- Mystic nature religion that evolved into a veneration of the island of Japan itself as the center of creation with its leaders as the descendants of the gods.
- The purpose of the religion at one time was to promote Japanese supremacy. (stopped after WWII)
- Shrines and temples are devoted mainly to ancestor worship today.

4. Buddhism
(India, China, world)

Founder - Siddhartha Gautama (563-480 BC), The Enlightened One, Buddha.

Main ideas:

- There is no one personal supreme being.

- Life is a mixture of spirits, gods, beings that are all in a continuous process of becoming part of the "whole."

- The "State of Nirvana" is reached when a person ceases to desire a conscious independent life and is fully absorbed into the whole.

- Like a drop of water is absorbed into the ocean, it ceases to be itself and becomes part of the ocean, the whole.

- Meditation, yoga, self-denial, study leads to Nirvana.

Eastern Religions (India)

1. Hinduism (India)

- Oldest organized religion still practiced today - 2000 BC.

- No founder. Evolved from nature religion to a social system that produced 4 strata or castes in Indian society with the priestly or religious leaders at the top.

- Similar to Buddhism in that the goal of life is complete oblivion (Moksha) and merging with Brahma (ultimate life power).

- Good deeds, self-denial, yoga, avoiding bad karma helps the soul reach Moksha. It may take several lifetimes in several forms (animals and human) before the soul reaches this state (reincarnation).

2. Jainism (India)

Founder - Nataputta Vardhamana (599-527 AD)

Main ideas:

- Similar to both Hinduism & Buddhism in that the goal is Moksha, Nirvana. Difference is twofold:
    - Only way to reach it was self-discipline and self-denial - not knowledge. (Jain means "to conquer")
    - Once reached however, the individual becomes part of the whole but not completely oblivious, he still has consciousness.
- Founder starved himself to death after claiming to have reached Moksha in his lifetime.

3. Sikhism (Pakistan)

Founder - Nanak (1469-1558 AD)

Main ideas:

- Lived in an area bordering Hindus and Muslims.
- Combination of Hindu and Muslim ideas (Moksha and reincarnation, Hinduism / Monotheism, Muslim).
- One reaches Moksha through love of God and doing good. Moksha is a conscious experience.
- Rejected Hindu "caste" system, equal society, believed in the brotherhood of all men.
- Ruled by a succession of "Gurus," the last of which (Govind Singh) required all devotees to add Singh (lion) to their names and carry the 5 K's: 1. Kesh (long hair) 2. Kangha (comb) 3. Kachh (shorts) 4. Kara (steel bracelet) 5. Kirpan (sword)

Near Eastern Religions (Middle East)

So far we have looked at religions that are not too familiar to us in the West. As we begin the Near Eastern religions we'll be reviewing groups that we know more about - well, except this 1st Near Eastern religion.

1. Zoroastrianism (Iran)

Founder - Zoroaster (660-583 BC)

Main ideas:

- Based on the visions of Zoroaster.

- Monotheist taught that doing good and avoiding evil brought one to God in heaven.

- Used fire in their worship system.

- Believed that God sent a special envoy every 1000 years called a "Sadshyant."

- Some think that the "Wise Men" who visited Jesus were Zoroastrians.

- Only a few thousand left, mostly in Mumbai (former Bombay) area of India.

2. Islam (Saudi Arabia, world)

Founder - Mohammed (570-632 AD)

Main ideas:

- Based on the visions of Mohammed and writing of these in the Koran as the final word of God.

- Man goes to Paradise through complete submission to God.

- Submission is exercised through practice of "5 Pillars"

  1. Confession - repeating phrase "There is no God but Allah and Mohammed is his prophet"

  2. Alms giving - 2% income

  3. Prayer - 5 times per day

  4. Fasting - during holy month, "Ramadan"

  5. Pilgrimage - trip to Mecca in Saudi Arabia

Originally spread through military means. Different groups within Islam often in conflict with each other: Sunnis, Shiites, Sufiis, Bahai, Black Muslims and Islam Nation.

3. Judaism (Israel, world)

Founder - Abraham (approx. 2000 BC)

Main ideas:

- Earliest of truly monotheistic religions.

- God has chosen the Jewish race to be his special representatives and will bless the world through them.

- Keeping God's laws (contained in Jewish scriptures given to Moses, prophets, etc.) keeps you as God's people and blessed here on earth.

- No consistent view of afterlife.

- Main temple used for worship in Jerusalem destroyed in 70 AD.

- Synagogues now used for assembly, prayer, singing, readings.

Modern Judaism has three main groups:

- Reform Judaism - liberal branch. Reconcile beliefs to modern science and society. Promote modern state of Israel.

- Conservative Judaism - still hold to concept of Messiah or personal Savior to come.

- Orthodox Judaism - hold to historical practice and beliefs of ancient Judaism except for animal sacrifices. Extremely conservative in dress and religious law.

4. Christianity (Israel, world)

Founder - Jesus Christ (4 BC - 29 AD+)

Main ideas:

- Jesus Christ is the promised Messiah/Savior of the Jewish religion.

- He is the embodiment of God in human form, and thus his teachings and commands have divine authority.

- He performed public miracles and was executed by the Roman government.

- He rose from the dead after three days, appeared to His disciples for 40 days and then ascended to heaven.

- Christianity believes that the death of Christ pays mankind's moral debt before God and people are saved from judgment by faith in Jesus and will live a conscious eternal life with God.

In brief form, these are the summaries that describe the world's 11 major religions.

The Supremacy of the Christian Religion

Now most of this chapter has dealt with the description of the major religions that exist today. I would like to finish chapter 2 by listing three reasons why Christianity is the superior religion among all religions, including the primitive ones discussed previously.

#1 - Christianity has a superior revelation of God.

Most religions have a very limited view of God as either an impersonal force or a kind of super-human being. Christianity reveals that God is pure Spirit with consciousness, will, power, knowledge, moral force and communicative power. Christianity explains what kind of being God is as well as what He wants from us and for us.

#2 - Christianity has a Superior Leader.

All other religions have men or women as leaders, prophets, gurus, priests, etc. Christianity has God Himself as leader in the form of a human being, Jesus Christ. In the Christian religion the leader is always alive and present to direct and encourage His followers in every generation.

#3 - Christianity offers a superior solution to the problems of humanity.

Other religions offer to solve humanity's problem by imposing religious rules or practices, or a final solution after death occurs. Christianity on the other hand:

A. Identifies the underlying problem causing human suffering.

Separation from God because of disobedience to God's laws (sin) leads to guilt, shame, rebellion, death, judgment, and condemnation.

B. Provides a solution for the problem.

God Himself takes the responsibility for paying off mankind's moral debt through the sacrificial death of Jesus Christ.

- In Christianity, God does for humans what humans cannot do for themselves. He eliminates guilt by eliminating the moral debt caused by sin.

- In Christianity people do not find salvation based on their ability to practice their religion or observe moral codes, (as is the case in every other organized religion).

- In Christianity God Himself, through Jesus Christ, saves people based on their faith in Him.

The practice of their religion and the keeping of moral codes are ongoing expressions of that faith but not the dynamic that ultimately saves them.

C. Christianity offers a better hope.

Far Eastern and Eastern religions' best offer is that the individuals cease to be at death or sooner. Islam and Judaism offer a Paradise that is much like here on earth, only better. In many respects this is what primitive religions also offer: safety here, ideal situation after death. Christianity, however, offers its followers the hope that while they are alive here on earth they can expect:

- Freedom from guilt and fear
- Peace of mind
- Loving relationships with other believers
- Greater insight into the mind of God
- A spiritual renewal

In addition to these things Christians can look forward to an afterlife where they are:

- Conscious spirits with personal identity

- Free from physical limits including death and sin

- Joined to God in an intimate personal relationship for eternity

There are many more reasons we can argue why Christianity is superior:

- Greatest number of followers.

- Most historical written records.

- Eyewitness accounts of Jesus' life.

- Positive impact of Christianity in the world, etc.

But I have only given a few in this chapter to highlight the superior nature of Christianity's claims. In our remaining 5 chapters we will examine more closely the Christian faith and the lifestyle of those who practice it.

#2 - The Christian Religion
Discussion Questions

Why do you think that there are so many similarities between the major religions in the world including Christianity?

What one thing, in your opinion, makes Christianity superior to other religions? Why?

Why does God permit so many religions to exist and grow?

3.
THE BIBLE

In this chapter we will examine three main things about the Bible including its content, its history and its claims.

Bible Content and History

It is very difficult to study the content of the Bible without describing some of its history as well, so we will review both of these ideas together in order to understand not only what is in the Bible but how it came to be written as well. The story of the recording of the Bible as a written record is the story of God's communication to man.

The Origin of the Bible

The word Bible comes from the Greek word, Biblia which means "books." The complete Bible/books numbers 66 (39 in the Old Testament and 27 in the New Testament). To study Bible origin we must begin with the Old Testament or a better word is Old Covenant. This term is very useful because it helps us understand what the Bible is: the details of two covenants or agreements between God and man. The old one and the new one which replaces the old (like a lease where certain changes are made when renewing).

Old Testament Origin

Our study of the Bible requires us to understand several features of the Old Testament. It was written in the Hebrew language which is still used today in Israel. The first man charged with actually recording events and communication from God was Moses (1500 BC).

- Exodus 24:1-4   - words of covenant at Sinai.
- Exodus 34:27-28 - 10 commandments.

Moses is credited with writing and organizing the first 5 books of the Bible called the Pentateuch (Joshua 8:31). Jesus confirms this in Matthew 4:4. Once God began to use human beings to record His words, this system continued after Moses.

- Joshua was the next writer after Moses
  - Joshua 24:26.
- Prophets recorded their history and prophecies after Joshua - Nehemiah 8:18.

In this way over a period of 1500 years, approximately 28 writers completed the 39 books of the Old Testament.

Malachi was the last to record in 516 BC. There were no other prophets sent to Israel until John the Baptist.

All these books were collected and assembled together into one volume by 400 BC and the Jews had a complete "Bible" 300 years before Christ.

Old Testament Organization

The Jews had the same Old Testament as we do but they organized it a little differently. They divided the Old Testament into 3 main sections:

1. **The Law** - Genesis-Deuteronomy. This was the highest in importance.

2. **The Prophets**
   Former - Joshua, Judges, Samuel
   Latter - Isaiah, Jeremiah, Lamentations, Ezekiel
   Minor - (book of 12) in one volume.

3. **The (Holy) Writings** - Poetry, History (Job, Psalms, Proverbs, etc. Esther-Nehemiah; Daniel).

They organized these into 24 books instead of our usual 39 books.

- Pentateuch – Genesis to Deuteronomy   = 5 books
- Prophets – Former + Latter + Minor   = 8 books
- Writings – Poetry/History   = 11 books

Total 24 books

Today we have the same books but they are divided differently:

- Pentateuch – Genesis to Deuteronomy   = 5 books
- History – Joshua to Esther   = 12 books
- Poetry – Job to Song of Solomon   = 5 books
- Major Prophets – Isaiah to Daniel   = 5 books
- Minor Prophets – Hosea to Malachi   = 12 books

Total 39 books

The Old Testament Story

Of course how many books and how they are divided does not tell us what the Old Testament is about. Even though the material was collected and written over a 1,500 year period and recorded by more than 25 different authors, the Old Testament of the Bible tells only one unbroken story - God's relationship with mankind, and in particular one certain group. In Genesis we have an account of the creation of the world and how the environment, society, and human beings came to be in their present state:

- A ruined natural world.

- A dysfunctional society.

- Humans doomed to die.

In Genesis we also read about a man called Abraham, chosen by God to be the head of a nation through whom God would offer salvation to all. The rest of the Old Testament books describe the growth and development of this man's family from a wandering tribe to a powerful and wealthy nation called Israel.

Most of the Old Testament books will contain information on their wars, conquests, politics, religion, moral codes, poetry and general history. It will also contain prophecies (predictions) of future events that will happen to their nation as well as the appearance and work of the savior originally promised to Abraham.

Although complicated to read at times, the Old Testament is really one story describing God's relationship with the Jewish people and their role in preparing a cultural and historical stage for the appearance of Jesus Christ.

New Testament Origin

The New Testament, like the Old, is also a story given in various books. The story it tells is of the life, ministry, death, burial, and resurrection of Jesus Christ and the subsequent spread of His teachings by His followers (Apostles) who established the Christian church in the 1st century. There were many accounts written of Jesus' life but the New Testament canon ("official" or "inspired" books) has only 27 books. I will explain how these came to be in a moment, but the division is as follows:

- Gospels - Matthew, Mark, Luke, John   = 4 books

- History - Book of Acts of the Apostles   = 1 book

- Pauline Epistles   = 13 books
  Letters written by Paul (Romans, 1-2 Corinthians, Galatians, Ephesians, Philippians, Colossians, 1-2 Thessalonians, 1-2 Timothy, Titus, Philemon)

- General Epistles   = 8 books
  (Hebrews, James, 1-2 Peter, 1-3 John, Jude)

- Prophecy – Revelation   = 1 book

Total 27 books

Aside from the gospels (accounts of Jesus' life) and Acts (history of the establishment of the church) most of the other letters were written to churches in order to teach and encourage them in the practice of their Christian faith. They applied and completed the original teachings of Christ. What is of great interest to many, however, is how this ancient material came to us today in this number and in our own language?

New Testament Canon

Many books were written about the life of Jesus and several books were written by the Apostles and their disciples. How did they decide which books actually belonged in the New Testament? The books that make up the New Testament are called the canon - from a Greek word which means "measuring rod." The word referred to those things which measured up when examined.

In other words, when the early church examined all the material that was written about Jesus, how did they decide which books belonged in the New Testament canon? Out of the hundreds of books, letters, etc. how did they narrow down to 27? There were 3 main factors that led the early church to form the New Testament canon and preserve it in one book.

In the beginning the church did not have a high regard for keeping the letters of the Apostles and the disciples. The apostles were alive and producing many letters so there was no urgency in preserving them. There was a lot of written material being produced so no one thought that they needed to keep some of it. They also thought Jesus was coming back in their lifetime so the need for preserving the material for the future was not there.

But then certain events took place that required them to begin collecting and preserving the teachings of the Lord and Apostles:

Canon of Marcion - 140 AD

Marcion was a false teacher who rejected the entire Old Testament, accepted only ten of the epistles of Paul and a part of Luke's gospel but rejected the others. He began circulating this group as the official canon and so the early church was forced to decide which of the writings were authoritative, and decided to collect and circulate these. This was done in 170 AD.

Persecution

Under the Roman Emperor Diocletian, it was a capital offense to possess a copy, any copy, of the Christian Scriptures. This brought up the question - which scriptures were worth dying for? Many uninspired, historical books were burned and only the most precious, most accepted works were kept.

Codex Form

Codex is the "book" form where several pages were placed together instead of using a scroll. When the codex form became popular, it brought up the question, which books should be grouped together into one volume. This motivated them to keep only the books that were acceptable in a single volume.

But the main question for the early church was "Which are the inspired books?"

There was no meeting where they reviewed all the material and then made a decision as to which made it in and which did not. On the contrary, the early church simply accepted those works that had already been recognized as inspired over the centuries but had not yet been collected and organized into one set. This was finally done in 367 AD and the 27 books confirmed by the Council of Carthage later in that century has remained the same since, without a single change. But in collecting the books for inclusion in the New Testament canon, the early church was guided by certain principles:

Authorship

If a man was inspired when he spoke, then his writings were also considered inspired. For this reason the writings of the Apostles were quickly accepted into the canon. Also the men associated with the Apostles were accepted. Luke was accepted because of his association with Paul. Mark was accepted because of his association with Peter. James was called the brother of the Lord and an Apostle (Galatians 1:19).

This allowed the gospels and the letters of Paul, Peter, James and John to be a natural selection for the Canon.

Value of Book

In some cases a book had a name attached to it but did not read like a New Testament book. For example, many uninspired authors tried to gain an audience by putting the name of an Apostle on their book: Acts of Peter (not written by Peter).

Scholars tell us that it was fairly easy to distinguish between inspired and fake when you actually read the material. For example, The Gospel of Thomas: Jesus made sparrows out of mud, was rebuked for doing this on the Sabbath and said "rise up and fly away" and the birds came to life and flew away.

There is another story where Jesus miraculously lengthened a board to fit a table being made in Joseph's shop. In other words, when comparing the writings, it was fairly easy to tell the real from the fakes. The inspired books had harmony of thought, purpose, and style. There were no contradictions and were accurate historically as well as theologically.

Circulation

The church did not decide which ones were suitable and which ones were not, they merely confirmed and collected those books which had traditionally been accepted by all the churches but had never been collected into one volume before.

No new book was introduced, only those letters and volumes that had wide circulation and acceptance after long ages of study and review.

The Canon was confirmed 300 years after the first writings began to be circulated. We also believe that God was guiding and protecting the process in which His word was recorded and preserved.

New Testament Translations

The Old Testament was written in the Hebrew language (most of it - some small parts in Aramaic). There came a time when the Jews could not speak Hebrew because of the Greek influence and so a translation of the Hebrew Old Testament was made in the Greek language. It was called the Septuagint because 70 scholars were used to create it. During New Testament times the people spoke Aramaic, which was an ancient language of Palestine. The books and letters of the New Testament were not written in the Aramaic language. They were written in the common form of Koine Greek, which was the universal language of the period. The Greek form remained the standard as copies were made from the original and distributed for the first several centuries.

There are in existence today 5,357 Greek manuscripts of portions of the New Testament. Scholars work with more copies of the New Testament than copies of the original Greek tragedies or copies of the writings of Shakespeare.

With time, the Greek was translated into Latin and other languages but these translations were always made from the original Greek manuscripts, not from Greek to Latin to German to English but always from the Greek.

Latin was the language of the Western portion of the Roman Empire and as Christianity spread westward from its original home (where Greek was the dominant language) a new version of the Bible was developed.

In 404 AD a new Latin version of the Bible was produced by Jerome, an early church leader. His translation from the Greek to Latin was called the Latin Vulgate. This became the standard version for study and church life in the middle ages.

Various translations were made into "common" languages of the time from the 5th-14th centuries that included Gothic, Syrian, Slavic, English, French, German, Italian and Spanish. By the 14th century there was a renewed interest in the Greco-Roman world's languages and literature, which were sparked by the Renaissance. This produced a greater effort to examine the Greek language.

This new trend led to a revival of the study of Greek and Hebrew languages as well as a study of the ancient Biblical manuscripts. This zeal to produce new Bible versions in common languages translated directly from the original Greek and Hebrew was helped along by the new religious movement called the Reformation. With the invention of Gutenberg's printing press in 1436 the technology to actually produce mass quantities of Bibles in different languages was realized.

It is interesting to note that the very first book to be printed on Gutenberg's new invention was the Latin Vulgate version of the Bible sometime between 1452 and 1456. This Bible was called the 42 line Bible because there were exactly 42 lines on each page. It still exists today and can be seen at the Gutenberg Museum in Mainz (near Frankfort), Germany.

The invention of the printing press helped spread the Bible in various languages throughout the world. The earliest known English translation was in 700 AD. A Latin version with English notes between the lines.

- John Wycliffe did the first complete English translation in 1382. He was imprisoned for his efforts.

- William Tyndale translated the first printed English Bible in 1526. Tyndale is a large religious publishing house today.

There were many translations as the science of translation and archaeology developed. One major translation was the King James Bible in 1611 and it became the authorized version for English speaking people for many years. It is still one of the most popular Bible translations today.

Many other translations have appeared over the years and each has a different style. For example:

- **Revised Standard Version** - good Old Testament but New is a little awkward.

- **American Standard** - best word per word translation but English is complicated.

- **New American Standard** - most accurate to the original but easy to read.

- **New International Version** - English flows well but some find it too general.

- **New Living Translation** - newest one using easy to read modern English. Its goal is to give the most exact meaning using today's English.

There are many other translations but these are major ones.

Bible Claims

We have looked at the content of the Bible, how it came to be written and organized, as well as how the various translations were produced. One final point to consider is the Bible's major claim. In other words, "what does it say about itself?"

Very simply, the Bible claims that it is inspired, meaning that God is the author of the Bible. Humans simply wrote what He wanted and guided them to write.

> All Scripture is inspired by God …
> - II Timothy 3:16a
>
> [20] But know this first of all, that no prophecy of Scripture is a matter of one's own interpretation, [21] for no prophecy was ever made by an act of human will, but men moved by the Holy Spirit spoke from God.
> - II Peter 1:20-21

Now it is easy to make claims but why do Christians believe the claim that the Bible is not just a book written by good and holy men but is in fact fully inspired by God? There are many reasons and we will briefly look at three:

1. Its ability to survive

Despite every effort to discredit its teachings and claims by governments, religious organizations, philosophers and skeptics of every kind for almost 2000 years - the Bible has survived intact. And despite constant attacks it continues to be the most translated, most printed, most read book in the world and in all of history. Of course you would expect no less from a book that says that it comes from God. Another reason Christians believe the Bible is from God…

2. Its uniqueness

One reason why many religions come and go is that their teachings are demonstrated to be false or become irrelevant in the modern world. The Christian religion and the Bible as its source however are unique among religious books.

- Unique in its depth and insight compared to any other secular or religious book: scholars agree.

- Unique in its unity: 66 books, 1500 years to write, 40 different authors and yet it is perfectly fitted together without contradiction telling a single story seamlessly.

- Unique in its universality in that it is read and followed by every culture and language and perfectly adaptable in every time period, ancient or modern.

Only a book with a Divine source could lay claim to such unique features. There are other reasons to believe the Bible's claim that it is inspired of God but one last one I would like to touch on is:

3. Fulfilled prophecy

Humans cannot accurately predict future events. To be able to do so is a sign of Divine power, to do so 100% of the time is a sure proof that God is at work. The Bible contains hundreds of such prophecies. Events, people, situations described by prophets, kings, teachers that were fulfilled years or even centuries later.

> "It is I who says of Cyrus, 'He is My shepherd!
> And he will perform all My desire.'
> And he declares of Jerusalem, 'She will be built,'
> And of the temple, 'Your foundation will be laid.'"
> - Isaiah 44:28

Isaiah lived in 700 BC. Cyrus, the king he names, lived 100 years later and history records this fact. The prophet names him, gives his position, and what he will do. We know from Isaiah and from history that everything that was prophesied actually happened.

> ^{32} They were on the road going up to Jerusalem, and Jesus was walking on ahead of them; and they were amazed, and those who followed were fearful. And again He took the twelve aside and began to tell them what was going to happen to Him, ^{33} saying, "Behold, we are going up to Jerusalem, and the Son of Man will be delivered to the chief priests and the scribes; and they will condemn Him to death and will hand Him over to the Gentiles. ^{34} They will mock Him and spit on Him, and scourge Him and kill Him, and three days later He will rise again."
> - Mark 10:32-34

Jesus predicts who will condemn Him, how He will be killed, and in how many days He will rise. Accurate prediction and fulfillment of future events is a definite sign that a supernatural force is at work. Only God can do this and He has done it in the Bible. In addition to this, the Bible is the only book, Holy or otherwise, that contains accurately fulfilled prophecies. No other book or writings in other religions have or claim this.

If the Bible is inspired, as it claims to be, you would expect that it would contain features only possible through divine power.

Well, that is our chapter reviewing the content, history, and claims of the Bible, the book that Christians use as their guide. In our next chapter we will examine the focus of the Bible records, Jesus Christ Himself.

#3 - The Bible
Discussion Questions

Does the Bible have to be inspired to be influential? Why?

How do we answer people who say that a 2000-year-old book is not relevant in today's society?

Which of the arguments for the Bible's super-natural source are strongest? Weakest? Why?

4.
JESUS CHRIST

This chapter will examine the person of Jesus Christ who is the reason for our faith. There are many theories about Jesus:

- He was an ancient Jewish rabbi.

- He was just a prophet of some kind.

- He was a ghost or spirit.

- Some have even said that He was some kind of alien being from another planet or some kind of advanced life form.

I am sure the speculation will continue and more opinions and theories will eventually be developed. For Christians, however, the only source for information about Jesus, His life, ministry, teachings - is the Bible. So this chapter should really be entitled, "What does the Bible say about Jesus?" This is the best way to discover who Jesus is because only the Bible contains eyewitness accounts of His life recorded and preserved for us to read even to this day.

The Bible's Central Theme

In the previous chapter I explained how the Bible was written, how it was organized, and why Christians believe that it comes from God. In this chapter we will discuss the major theme of the Bible.

The entire Bible is about Jesus.

He is the main point of all the books of the Bible. The different parts explain different things about Him and His interaction with us.

1. The Old Testament is really the story about the creation of the world and how God prepared for His coming by the forming of the Jewish nation. It contains all the events that set a human and historical stage for His eventual appearance as a man in this world. It tells this story through the eyes and words of Jewish prophets, leaders, and kings.

2. The 4 gospels are the eyewitness accounts of His life, ministry, death, resurrection, and ascension to heaven. Again, the story recorded and preserved by men who were with Him for years and who knew Him intimately.

3. The rest of the New Testament, written by other Apostles and their disciples, shows how His followers established the Christian church according to His instructions. In addition to this there are teachings to help followers/disciples live their Christian lives in every generation and environment.

We could go anywhere in the Bible to find out about Jesus concerning:

- The promise of His coming
- The preparation for His appearance
- The circumstances of His miraculous birth
- The content of His teachings
- The details of His death and resurrection
- The people who knew Him personally and spread His teachings throughout the world

I do not think we would have the time in a single chapter to do all this. What we can do, however, is to focus on what the Bible says about who Jesus is. This is actually the most important question about Jesus Christ and we will see what three individuals, mentioned in the Bible, say about Jesus.

Who is Jesus?

Now remember we are asking the question, "Who is Jesus?" according to the Bible, not just what we think or feel or learned from a book or movie or teacher of some kind. Since most of the direct and eyewitness accounts about Him are in the New Testament portion of the Bible, let us go there to learn about Him. Thousands of people saw and heard Jesus speak, teach, and even do miracles. There is no doubt of His existence because historians of that era write about Him and His ministry.

Josephus Flavius, who was a Jewish historian, wrote about this period. He was not a follower of Jesus but mentions Him and Christianity in general in his history books. History (not the Bible) writes that Jesus was a Jewish man born into a humble family who lived in Israel approximately 2000 years ago. He began His ministry by claiming that He was the

Jewish Messiah or Savior and was eventually arrested and executed by the Roman government at the insistence of the Jewish leaders who accused Him of causing civil unrest by His teaching. Eventually His followers established the Christian church based on His teachings. This is what history books teach about the facts of His life.

Witness of the Apostles

There were others, however, who actually followed Jesus as His special disciples and they too recorded their accounts of His life. It is from these writers, whose records form the New Testament, that we can establish a much more comprehensive picture of who Jesus really was. For the sake of our study we will examine three of these men's writings and descriptions of Jesus.

1. Peter

Peter was a fisherman by trade and along with his brother Andrew, had a family business. He was the first "Apostle" called by Jesus to follow Him on a full time basis. He was to hear all of Jesus' teachings, witness His miracles, and later on be a leader in establishing the church and finally die as a martyr in Rome claiming to the very end that what he heard and saw was true.

During Jesus' ministry, Jesus asked the Apostles (including Peter), based on what they saw Him say and do, who did they think He was? And Peter answered without hesitation, "You are the Messiah the son of the Living God." (Matthew 16:16) So the Bible says that even while Jesus was alive Peter believed and declared Him to be the divine Son of God.

Later on, after Jesus was executed, Peter describes the things that he saw with his own eyes as he rebukes the Jews for their hard hearts and disbelief.

> [14] But you disowned the Holy and Righteous One and asked for a murderer to be granted to you,
> [15] but put to death the Prince of life, the one whom God raised from the dead, a fact to which we are witnesses.
> - Acts 3:14-15

Now there is much written about Peter in the New Testament and Peter himself writes two of the books or epistles contained in this part of the Bible, but just these two passages summarize well what Peter thought about Jesus based on what he experienced:

- That Jesus was the Christ/Messiah/Savior promised in the Old Testament. In other words, Jesus was the one sent by God to save mankind.

- Peter also concluded that Jesus was divine, based on what he heard Jesus say and saw Him do.

- Finally, Peter saw Jesus executed by Roman soldiers and then saw Him after God raised Him from the dead.

As I said before, Peter never changed or denied this witness, even when he was threatened, imprisoned, and finally sent to his death for saying these things. So when we want to know who Jesus is, the Bible through Peter's words says that He is the Son of God, the Savior, and He is resurrected from the dead.

2. Thomas

Another Apostle we know less about was Thomas, he is the one often referred to as "doubting Thomas" because he wanted proof of Jesus' resurrection before he would believe. What he says about Jesus is interesting because of this very fact: he demanded proof before he would continue to believe.

- He knew Jesus and, like the other Apostles, had lived and worked with Jesus for 3 years.

- He saw the miracles, heard the teachings and witnessed Jesus die on the cross.

- He was convinced Jesus was dead, so brutal and final was His execution at the hands of the Roman soldiers.

- When the other Apostles reported that they had seen Jesus resurrected and alive again, Thomas was skeptical and refused to believe.

In the gospel of John we read about Jesus' confrontation with Thomas to believe.

> [24] But Thomas, one of the twelve, called Didymus, was not with them when Jesus came. [25] So the other disciples were saying to him, "We have seen the Lord!" But he said to them, "Unless I see in His hands the imprint of the nails, and put my finger into the place of the nails, and put my hand into His side, I will not believe." [26] After eight days His disciples were again inside, and Thomas with them. Jesus came, the doors having been shut, and stood in their midst and said, "Peace be with you." [27] Then He said to Thomas, "Reach here with your finger, and see My hands; and reach here your hand and put it into My side; and do not be unbelieving, but believing." [28] Thomas answered and said to Him, "My Lord and my God!"
> - John 20:24-28

Note what this exchange teaches us about Jesus:

1. Thomas believes that Jesus is actually risen from the dead.

2. Thomas acknowledges that Jesus is God, not just a prophet or teacher or holy man.

3. The Apostle demonstrates that Jesus is worthy of not only belief, but worship as well.

4. Thomas, in calling Jesus Lord, indicates that Jesus has authority over him.

Once again, a short passage, but one where the Bible sets forth important facts about who Jesus is: divine, object of belief and worship, Lord over us. People are free to choose whether they believe this or not but the fact remains that this is what the Bible teaches about Jesus.

3. Paul

Perhaps no one, other than Jesus Himself, articulates in more detail the character or person of Jesus Christ than Paul the Apostle. Paul was a Jew and an early persecutor of the Christian church. As a Pharisee he was part of the ruling class in the Jewish society of Jesus' day. He was a religious zealot for Judaism who had obtained a mandate from the ruling council of Jewish leaders to wage a campaign of persecution against Christians in order to discourage their growth. In recounting his own experience Paul describes the meeting with Jesus Christ that changed his life.

> [1] "Brethren and fathers, hear my defense which I now offer to you." [2] And when they heard that he was addressing them in the Hebrew dialect, they became even more quiet; and he said, [3] "I am a Jew, born in Tarsus of Cilicia, but brought up in this city, educated under Gamaliel, strictly according to

the law of our fathers, being zealous for God just as you all are today. [4] I persecuted this Way to the death, binding and putting both men and women into prisons, [5] as also the high priest and all the Council of the elders can testify. From them I also received letters to the brethren, and started off for Damascus in order to bring even those who were there to Jerusalem as prisoners to be punished.

[6] "But it happened that as I was on my way, approaching Damascus about noontime, a very bright light suddenly flashed from heaven all around me, [7] and I fell to the ground and heard a voice saying to me, 'Saul, Saul, why are you persecuting Me?' [8] And I answered, 'Who are You, Lord?' And He said to me, 'I am Jesus the Nazarene, whom you are persecuting.' [9] And those who were with me saw the light, to be sure, but did not understand the voice of the One who was speaking to me. [10] And I said, 'What shall I do, Lord?' And the Lord said to me, 'Get up and go on into Damascus, and there you will be told of all that has been appointed for you to do.' [11] But since I could not see because of the brightness of that light, I was led by the hand by those who were with me and came into Damascus.

[12] "A certain Ananias, a man who was devout by the standard of the Law, and well spoken of by all the Jews who lived there, [13] came to me, and standing near said to me, 'Brother Saul, receive your sight!' And at that very time I looked up at him. [14] And he said, 'The God of our fathers has appointed you to know His will and to see the Righteous One and to hear an utterance from His mouth. [15] For you will be a witness for Him to all men of what you have seen and heard. [16] Now why do you delay? Get up and be baptized, and wash

away your sins, calling on His name.'
- Acts 22:1-16

And thus began the conversion and mission of one of the most prolific of Jesus' Apostles. We know both from history and the Bible that Paul went on to preach and establish the Christian religion throughout the Roman Empire. He was eventually imprisoned by the Emperor Nero and executed in Rome in 67 AD on account of his role as a Christian leader.

Paul, the adversary of the church, the one who initially denied who Jesus was, ended up giving his life for his faith in Christ. In his writings we have a very dynamic description of Jesus and His exalted position.

[15] He is the image of the invisible God, the firstborn of all creation. [16] For by Him all things were created, both in the heavens and on earth, visible and invisible, whether thrones or dominions or rulers or authorities—all things have been created through Him and for Him. [17] He is before all things, and in Him all things hold together. [18] He is also head of the body, the church; and He is the beginning, the firstborn from the dead, so that He Himself will come to have first place in everything.
- Colossians 1:15-18

Note what Paul specifically says about who Jesus is:

1. Visible image of God - When you see Jesus you're looking at God.

2. Existed before Creation - He exists before time, like God.

3. Supreme over Creation - He has the authority of God.

4. He is the agent of Creation - Everything in the material and spiritual world was created by and for Him.

5. He is Eternal - Another quality of God.

6. He is the head of the church - Jesus is the only leader of the church in heaven and on earth. He does not share this with any other person.

7. He leads those who will resurrect - Another way of saying He is eternal by saying He leads in the future – He is already there.

These things are not the only things Paul says about Jesus, but we can see from these that Paul was proclaiming Jesus as the divine Son of God based on his own experiences and knowledge of Christ and His teachings. So, we have reviewed three of the eyewitnesses who described and explained in the Bible who they believed Jesus to be.

The Testimony of Jesus

This leaves us with one last person to examine and that is Jesus Himself. Our description of Jesus would be incomplete if we did not examine at least a few things that Jesus said about His true identity. Here are three things He said about Himself to three individuals:

1. The Samaritan Woman

In a conversation with a woman while travelling Jesus answers her question about who is the true Messiah.

> 25 The woman said to Him, "I know that Messiah is coming (He who is called Christ); when that One comes, He will declare all things to us." 26 Jesus said to her, "I who speak to you am He."
> - John 4:25-26

Jesus describes Himself as the savior spoken of by the Jews.

2. Peter the Apostle

We have looked at Peter's declaration earlier in this chapter but this time let us focus on Jesus' response to what Peter says.

> [15] He said to them, "But who do you say that I am?" [16] Simon Peter answered, "You are the Christ, the Son of the living God." [17] And Jesus said to him, "Blessed are you, Simon Barjona, because flesh and blood did not reveal this to you, but My Father who is in heaven.
> - Matthew 16:15-17

Note that Jesus confirms what Peter says about Him and even goes on to reveal how Peter has come to this realization.

3. To the Apostles

After His resurrection and appearance to over 500 disciples, Jesus gives His Apostles (and future disciples) their mission.

> [18] And Jesus came up and spoke to them, saying, "All authority has been given to Me in heaven and on earth. [19] Go therefore and make disciples of all the nations, baptizing them in the name of the Father and the Son and the Holy Spirit, [20] teaching them to observe all that I commanded you; and lo, I am with you always, even to the end of the age."
> - Matthew 28:18-20

Note that in this passage Jesus claims exclusive divine authority over all. These are only a few of the things that are recorded concerning Jesus, but from these we see some of the things the Bible teaches about Him:

1. A true historical figure
2. The Jewish Messiah
3. The Son of God
4. The Lord God Himself
5. Resurrected from the dead
6. An eternal being
7. The agent of Creation
8. The head of the church
9. The supreme authority in heaven and earth

I could go on and on about what the Bible actually says concerning Jesus but I will close this chapter with a quote from the gospel of John who faced the similar dilemma of trying to list all the things he actually heard and saw Jesus do. Faced with the mountain of information before him John writes in the 20th and 21st chapters of his gospel record:

> [30] Therefore many other signs Jesus also performed in the presence of the disciples, which are not written in this book; [31] but these have been written so that you may believe that Jesus is the Christ, the Son of God; and that believing you may have life in His name.
> - John 20:30-31

> And there are also many other things which Jesus did, which if they were written in detail, I suppose that even the world itself would not contain the books that would be written.
> - John 21:25

#4 - Jesus Christ
Discussion Questions

Where is the best place to begin telling the story of Jesus? Why?

What was it about Jesus that led you to believe in Him? Share with your group.

Discuss the 3 major characteristics that best portray Jesus' divinity and why this is so.

5.
SALVATION

Every religion has their idea of salvation. This word usually refers to some altered or improved state of being in this life, or a new existence of some kind after death. Every religion, we have learned, has a different name for "salvation":

- The Taoists call it balance (ying/yang)

- Buddhists refer to it as nirvana

- Hindus call it Moksha

- Islam speaks of paradise

No matter what other religions call it or how they describe its experience, they all share a similar pathway to their own concepts of salvation.

In all religions, except Christianity, salvation is achieved by some kind of human effort.

For example, Buddhism requires meditation, knowledge and self-denial to reach its salvation goal. Islam demands that its adherents practice and maintain the five spiritual exercises if they wish to arrive at paradise. These are only two examples but all other religions (aside from Christianity) demand some form of moral or religious law keeping in order to become worthy and acceptable to a higher power and thus saved. The basic premise is always the same:

- Mankind is flawed and subject to death.

- God or a higher power/force provides the knowledge and method to improve this flawed condition and ultimately escape death in some way.

- That knowledge and method is mediated by religious leaders who teach and maintain the spiritual discipline to eventually be "saved."

- If the individual works hard enough, trains well enough, is zealous enough in his practice of religious customs and rules, he will win the prize: salvation.

Except for customs and names, this has been the pattern for obtaining salvation outlined by most of the major religions in the world throughout the history of mankind. Christianity's idea and approach to salvation is completely different.

Christianity and Salvation

Christianity begins with the same premise concerning mankind's general condition.

The Problem

Humans are flawed, subject to moral failure and physical suffering and death. The Bible, which reveals Christianity's view on human salvation, teaches that the source of this condition is mankind's sinfulness. Paul, the Apostle, summarizes this idea in his epistle to the Romans when he says:

> For all have sinned and fall short of the glory of
> God,
> - Romans 3:23

And then he declares what the consequence of this sinfulness is:

> For the wages of sin is death,
> - Romans 6:23a

In another epistle, John the Apostle, describes what sin is:

> Everyone who practices sin also practices
> lawlessness; and sin is lawlessness.
> - I John 3:4

In the book of Isaiah, the Old Testament prophet explains in more detail the effect that sin has on us and why it leads to death:

> But your iniquities have made a separation
> between you and your God,
> - Isaiah 59:2a

So if we were to summarize these few verses about sin and its effect we could say that:

- Sin is disobedience to God's will.

- Everyone at one time or another sins.

- This disobedience separates us from God.

- This separation ultimately leads to our physical death as well as our spiritual suffering because our spirit cannot be at peace or experience joy if it is separated from the Spirit of God in whose image it was originally created (Genesis 1:26).

Let me give you a visual example of this phenomenon:

> Let us say you have a plant. The main stem is God and the leaves are people. So long as the leaves are connected to the plant they are alive and produce more leaves and blossoms, etc. But if I were to separate a leaf from the main plant by cutting it off, what would happen? It would look the same, have the same color, even keep its freshness for a while.
>
> However, after a time it would dry up and die. That leaf would turn brown and eventually become dust, not capable of renewal. The main plant, however, and its leaves would continue to live and bloom.

This is not a perfect example but it does demonstrate the process that takes place through human sinfulness and the need for salvation (which is another word for "rescue"). We are born sinless and joined to God who brings us into being and sustains our physical and spiritual lives. Eventually we sin. We disobey His commands and laws concerning moral and spiritual behavior. In doing so we separate ourselves from Him and become subject to further moral decay, physical death, and a spiritual separation from God after death.

The problem here is that once we are cut off from God, we do not have the ability to reattach ourselves to Him, and thus are doomed just like the dead leaf cannot reattach itself to the plant. This is the essential difference between Christianity and all other religions. Other religions believe and teach that human beings are able to reattach themselves to God through human effort of some kind:

- Gaining religious knowledge and insight.
- Practicing religious disciplines such as worship, meditation, secret rituals, pilgrimages, etc.

- Some try to achieve it through extreme denial of human appetites, or food restrictions, etc.

Whatever the culture, tradition, or religion, the method is the same, an attempt to be reunited with God by human effort in order to avoid suffering, death, and the separation of the soul from its natural place with God. Christianity is unique in that it reveals a method for rescuing man based on God's actions and not human effort.

The Solution

The Bible teaches how God "rescues" or saves us from the death caused by our separation from Him due to our sins. Here is how it works:

God pays the moral debt we owe Him.

Each sin we make, each law we break creates a moral debt we owe to God. This moral debt is the cause of our guilt, shame, fear of death, and judgment because we know we are guilty. We cannot repay this moral debt because we are polluted by sin and cannot produce the sinless, perfect life required to remove a lifetime of imperfection and sin. God pays the moral debt through Jesus Christ, it is in this way that God "rescues" us. Paul, the Apostle, explains it this way:

> [6] For while we were still helpless, at the right time Christ died for the ungodly. [7] For one will hardly die for a righteous man; though perhaps for the good man someone would dare even to die. [8] But God demonstrates His own love toward us, in that while we were yet sinners, Christ died for us. [9] Much more then, having now been justified by His blood, we shall be saved from the wrath of God through Him. [10] For if while we were enemies we were

reconciled to God through the death of His Son, much more, having been reconciled, we shall be saved by His life. [11] And not only this, but we also exult in God through our Lord Jesus Christ, through whom we have now received the reconciliation.
- Romans 5:6-11

This passage explains and points out certain features of the Christian religion:

1. Why did God take on a human form in Jesus Christ?

Only a perfect life could be offered for the moral indebtedness of man and only God in the form of man could accomplish this perfect life.

2. Why did Jesus have to die in order to obtain this forgiveness for man's moral debt?

Death was required because according to God's spiritual laws, human sinfulness could only be atoned for through death. As the writer of the epistle to the Hebrews says,

And according to the Law, one may almost say, all things are cleansed with blood, and without shedding of blood there is no forgiveness.
- Hebrews 9:22

A perfect life was required to make up for the imperfect life of mankind destroyed by sin. God takes the form of a human being, Jesus Christ, and offers this innocent and perfect life as a sacrifice to pay the moral debt of sin for all of mankind.

3. How does the sacrifice of one pay for the sins of all?

If Jesus were only a man, a good and holy man, his sacrifice could atone for himself or another. One man pays for one other person. But because Jesus is God, has a divine nature - the value of His life and thus sacrifice is different.

As God, the sacrifice of His divine life is able to pay for the sins of all mankind.

> For Christ also died for sins once for all, the just for
> the unjust, so that He might bring us to God,
> having been put to death in the flesh, but made
> alive in the spirit;
> - I Peter 3:18

4. What was the role of the Jewish people?

God chose one man, Abraham, and from him He created a special people. He gave them their religion, a country, laws, and formed their culture and history (read about this process in the Old Testament). The reason for this was to provide a religious, cultural, and historical stage on which He would appear as Jesus Christ. His purpose was to offer His life for the sins of mankind; the Jewish people were the vehicle used to make His human appearance and be the first to be offered salvation.

5. What is the role of the Bible?

The Bible is the inspired account of God's plan to save humanity through Jesus Christ. It records the beginning of the world but then focuses in on the forming of the Jewish people and continues to tell their story until the appearance of Jesus and follows with the eyewitness accounts of His death, burial, and resurrection. It ends with the history of the forming of His church and the spread of Christianity in the 1st century.

Its main theme, however, is the salvation of mankind through Jesus Christ. Paul the Apostle summarizes this idea in writing to a young minister when he says,

> and that from childhood you have known the sacred writings which are able to give you the wisdom that leads to salvation through faith which is in Christ Jesus.
> - II Timothy 3:15

And so, Christianity presents a unique way to deal with the consequences of human weakness and moral failure. Not by human effort and religious practice or attempts to achieve moral perfection, but God offers Himself through Jesus Christ as the payment for the debt of sins. In Christianity, God rescues us from death, from separation, from condemnation, because we do not have the power to do so. This is not to say that humans have no participation in the rescue. We do offer something to God, but it is the only thing we truly have to give to God and that is our faith.

This brings us to the second important teaching in the Bible concerning this subject.

Salvation is offered to man based on faith, not human effort.

In Christianity God does what is impossible for man, pay the moral debt for sin, and man does what is humanly possible, he trusts God. This is the sum of salvation. God offers man rescue from death and separation caused by sin and man believes and trusts in God to accomplish this on his behalf. This beautiful reconciliation is described in various ways in the Bible.

Therefore, having been justified by faith, we have
peace with God through our Lord Jesus Christ,
- Romans 5:1

For God so loved the world, that He gave His only
begotten Son, that whoever believes in Him shall
not perish, but have eternal life.
- John 3:16

If I were to go back to my example of "separation" with the
plant used earlier in the chapter; in Christianity it is as if God
takes the cut-off branch and reattaches it back to Himself.
People do this with plants and damaged trees all the time, it
is called grafting. They cut a wedge and reattach the severed
branch and hold it in place with some kind of wrapping.

In the same way God grafts us back into Himself and the
element that holds us into place, so to speak, is faith. This is
the key doctrine of the Christian religion: salvation by faith
through grace. In other words, because of God's kindness
(grace) He offers us salvation (rescue) based on our faith in
Jesus Christ and not based on personal goodness or human
effort.

Paul the Apostle says it this way:

[21] But now apart from the Law the righteousness of
God has been manifested, being witnessed by the
Law and the Prophets, [22] even the righteousness
of God through faith in Jesus Christ for all those
who believe; for there is no distinction;
- Romans 3:21-22

Of course there are many facets and details to the Christian
religion I have not mentioned here and will discuss in our
next two chapters, but the issue of salvation and how it is
produced by God and received by man is the core teaching
of the Bible and Christianity. Now there are some questions

that naturally arise from this teaching and what most of us already know about Christianity.

What is faith and what exactly are we to believe?

Belief, by simple definition, is to accept something as true. In Christianity we accept as true that Jesus Christ is the son of God. When challenged to believe, Peter, one of the Apostles, demonstrated the essence of Christian belief when he said, "You are the Messiah, the son of the Living God." in Matthew 16:16.

There are many other teachings and details of the Christian faith that one must know and understand and believe, however, for salvation's sake, the essential belief is what we believe about Jesus Christ. Of course this belief includes our trust that His death pays for our sins and our faith in Him makes us right before God.

What about repentance and baptism?

In the Bible, faith is almost always associated and accompanied by repentance and baptism. Repentance refers to a change of heart. A turning from disbelief and sin to belief and a desire to please and obey God. The English word, baptism, comes from a Greek word which means to plunge or immerse in water. In the Bible those who believed in Jesus expressed that faith through repentance and baptism.

For example, When Peter the Apostle preached about Jesus' death and resurrection he encouraged people to believe and when they responded to him and asked how they were to do this, he said,

> Peter said to them, "Repent, and each of you be baptized in the name of Jesus Christ for the

> forgiveness of your sins; and you will receive the
> gift of the Holy Spirit.
> - Acts 2:38

In another passage Paul describes what was said to him before he was baptized by a man called Ananias,

> Now why do you delay? Get up and be baptized,
> and wash away your sins, calling on His name.
> - Acts 22:16

To summarize, God offers salvation through the sacrifice of Jesus Christ. We accept that sacrifice for our sins by faith, that is, by believing that Jesus is the Son of God. And we express that faith, according to God's command, in repentance and baptism.

Who can become a Christian and when can a person be baptized?

Jesus answers this question when He spoke to His Apostles recorded in the gospel of Mark,

> [15] And He said to them, "Go into all the world and
> preach the gospel to all creation. [16] He who has
> believed and has been baptized shall be saved;
> but he who has disbelieved shall be condemned.
> - Mark 16:15-16

Jesus Himself says that the good news of salvation is for everyone. Anyone who believes and is baptized is saved, no exceptions based on color, race, education, gender, social position. However, He also makes clear that those who refuse to believe have no alternative way to be saved. This means that when we come to belief - then we should not hesitate to express that faith in the way God intended, through repentance and baptism.

73

As we close this chapter on salvation, let me encourage anyone reading this message to believe in Jesus and trust in the way of salvation that only He offers. If you have not yet expressed your faith in repentance and baptism then please do so as soon as you can.

#5 – Salvation
Discussion Questions

What is the most common view of salvation among the major religions and why have they come to this conclusion?

Why do you think many people have no "feeling" of lostness? What can be done to reveal this to them?

Why do you think some people abandon Christianity in order to become Muslims, Buddhists, or Hindus?

6.
THE CHURCH

Before we look at what the Bible says about the church, I would like to review several of the most popular misconceptions that people have concerning the Christian church.

Misconception #1 - The church is a building

This is the most common idea about the church, that it is simply a structure. People say, "I go to the church on Main St." or "Where is your church located?" They see the church as a thing, a place, a type of architecture devoted to a religious function.

Misconception #2 - The church is a human organization

Another name for this is denominationalism. In other words, the church is a group of people that are identified by a certain "brand" name. For example, Catholic church, Protestant church, Baptist or Pentecostal church. Each group has its characteristics, traditions, even styles of architecture for its buildings that identify and distinguish them from other "churches" or groups.

Misconception #3 - All churches are the same

This idea is based on the notion that one church is as good as the other because they are all doing the same thing, serving the same God. It is like McDonalds and Burger King, different names, different brands, but basically the same type of fast food restaurants serving the same food. When we examine what the Bible says about the church however, we see what the church really is and how inaccurate these misconceptions really are!

The Church in the Bible

The surest way to have the correct picture of the church is to consult the Bible. After all, the one who started the Christian church (Jesus) and the ones who established it in the first century (the Apostles) are all recorded in the New Testament part of the Bible. If we want to know about the church, therefore, we need to consult the source book for information about it: the New Testament. So let us deal with the misconceptions first:

#1 - The church is a building

Although most of the public worship of the church takes place in a building (even one that has a special type of architecture), the building itself is not a church. The church building is only a building used by the church.

#2 - The church is a human organization

Although the church is organized, it is not like a human organization. It has structure but is not identified like other groups that have certain names and compete with other groups for position and power.

#3 - All churches are the same

This misconception presupposes that there are many types of churches and that they basically all fulfill the same purpose. The Bible, however, teaches that there is really only one church and it does not compete or divide over itself.

Now the simplest way to describe the church is to identify what the original word for church referred to. We know that the New Testament was originally written in the Greek language and the Greek word translated into the English word "church" was the word "ekklesia." This word was a combination of two expressions: To call, out of. So the word literally meant "those who are called-out or gathered."

Among the Greeks it referred to a body of citizens "gathered" to discuss the affairs of state. It has also been translated into the English words "assembly" and "congregation." Jesus first uses the word "church" in Matthew 16:18 when He says, "I will build my church." When Jesus begins using this word He is referring to His disciples.

- He will "call out" disciples.

- He will build His assembly.

- He will build His congregation.

So, from the very beginning the church always referred to people, not buildings or organizations. Of course the church was not just any assembly, gathering, or congregation of people: The church was the assembly of people who were disciples of Jesus Christ. Or, you could say it this way: the church is the gathering of all those who are saved by faith in Jesus Christ.

The key thing to understand, therefore, is that the church is made up of people who have been saved and follow Jesus Christ as Lord. In the book of Acts, Luke describes this process when he recounts how Peter was preaching about

Jesus, His death and resurrection, and encouraging people to believe. Observe how Luke describes the formation of the church in this process.

> [36] Therefore let all the house of Israel know for certain that God has made Him both Lord and Christ—this Jesus whom you crucified."
>
> [37] Now when they heard this, they were pierced to the heart, and said to Peter and the rest of the apostles, "Brethren, what shall we do?" [38] Peter said to them, "Repent, and each of you be baptized in the name of Jesus Christ for the forgiveness of your sins; and you will receive the gift of the Holy Spirit. [39] For the promise is for you and your children and for all who are far off, as many as the Lord our God will call to Himself." [40] And with many other words he solemnly testified and kept on exhorting them, saying, "Be saved from this perverse generation!" [41] So then, those who had received his word were baptized; and that day there were added about three thousand souls.
> - Acts 2:36-41

Note how people become members of the church. The Gospel is preached. Those who believe and are baptized are saved (just as Jesus said they would be in Mark 16:16). They are added (joined to) the existing assembly (church) who have already been saved.

So the church is not a building, nor an organization you can join, nor is it one of many. The church is a group of people who have been called out of disbelief to belief in Jesus Christ and assembles together as one group.

This group exists on a worldwide basis as all those in history who have become Christians: these are the church. On a smaller scale, Christians who gather in local congregations in various places for worship and service, these also are the church. At its most basic level however, the church in the Bible refers to those who are saved by faith in Jesus Christ and obey His word as faithful disciples. And this is the church even if:

- They meet in an elaborate "church building" or someone's home.

- They call themselves by a specific "brand" name or use only the simple term Christian or disciple.

If you are a faithful follower of Jesus, you have been automatically added to His church, His assembly, His congregation.

Imagery of the Church

Even though the basic concept of the church is simple, how it functions and the role it plays in God's plan is complex and quite exalted. In the New Testament there are literally dozens of metaphors used to describe the church and how God sees its position and attributes in the spiritual realm.

I have chosen only 20 of these to highlight the value and beauty God accords to the assembly, the congregation, the church. I have put these in the order that they appear in the Bible. At its most basic level, the church is the gathering of all those who are saved by Christ. God has an exalted view and function for the church that reflects its importance and key role in accomplishing God's will.

Note that these word images are not meant to be "brand names" for different denominations, but rather ways to describe the many facets of the church's character and spiritual role in God's plan.

1.   Kingdom of Heaven - Matthew 3:2
2.   Kingdom of God - Matthew 6:33
3.   Church of God - Acts 20:28
4.   Church of Christ - Romans 16:16
5.   God's Field - I Corinthians 3:9
6.   God's Building - I Corinthians 3:9
7.   Heavenly Jerusalem - Galatians 4:26
8.   Israel of God - Galatians 6:16
9.   Body of Christ - Ephesians 1:22-23
10. Holy Temple - Ephesians 2:21
11. Dwelling Where God Lives - Ephesians 2:22
12. Household of God - I Timothy 3:15
13. Pillar and Ground of the Truth - I Timothy 3:15
14. Mt. Zion - Hebrews 12:22
15. City of the Living God - Hebrews 12:22
16. Church of the Firstborn - Hebrews 12:23
17. Flock of God - I Peter 5:2
18. Golden Lampstand - Revelation 1:21
19. New Jerusalem - Revelation 21:2
20. Bride and Wife of the Lamb - Revelation 21:9

I could go for pages describing the significance of each of these names and references, but suffice to say that they demonstrate the unique and spiritual character/gifts shared by each individual who makes up the "church" that Jesus builds.

Church Types

If you were to drive down any major street in any city you would soon notice that contrary to what the Bible teaches - there are many types of churches, not just one church as the Bible teaches. There are several reasons for this phenomenon:

1. Unbiblical foundation

The Bible determines what the church is, how it should function, and how it needs to be organized. Jesus and the Apostles left all the information about the church in the Bible and nowhere else. The Bible is the only legitimate blueprint or guidebook to establish and grow the church.

There are different "types" of churches because people insist on adding human ideas, traditions, teachings in the place of the Bible or in addition to the Bible. Every time you do this you create a variation of the original and with many changes and additions over the centuries there have also been a multiplication of the "types" of churches that come into being.

For example, take a clothing pattern that someone will use to make a shirt. If you follow the pattern you will produce the same shirt over and over again. However, if you change one thing in the pattern, like adding a second pocket, you will begin to have variations of the shirt. Your new creation will be a shirt but not one according to the original pattern.

In the same way, the Bible is the "pattern" for the church. If you follow its pattern you will produce the church of the Bible over and over in each generation and place. If you deviate from the Bible pattern you will create a variation. This is how new and different churches evolve.

Another reason why there are different types of churches is...

2. People do not agree on the meaning of the Bible

It is not something that Christians like to admit, but there is often disagreement about the meaning and application of certain texts in the Bible. Unfortunately, when two groups cannot agree on how to interpret or put into practice a certain teaching or passage of scripture, they form different groups in order to promote their point of view.

These separate groups often grow into separate churches with different identities and different traditions that have little to do with each other. This is why you have hundreds of different "types" of groups all claiming to be the "church" but having different practices and points of view on the variety of issues.

I believe that Jesus knew enough about human nature to know that this type of thing would happen in the church He was creating during His time on earth. This is why at the very beginning of the formation of the church, as He was calling out the very first disciples, He prayed for unity among His followers,

> Holy Father, keep them in Your name, the name which You have given Me, that they may be one even as We are.
> - John 17:11b

According to the Bible, the church is united in its love, its beliefs, its organization, its practice, its worship and service. Paul explained it this way in the letter to the Ephesian church,

> [3] being diligent to preserve the unity of the Spirit in the bond of peace. [4] There is one body and one Spirit, just as also you were called in one hope of your calling; [5] one Lord, one faith, one baptism, 6 one God and Father of all who is over all and through all and in all.
> - Ephesians 4:3-6

The pressure of division was already being felt in the 1st century church, but Paul holds forth the ideal of the church given to him by God in Christ. So there is only one church and it is perfectly united and created according to God's plan and purpose. The pattern for that "true" church is in the New Testament and God calls on every Christian in every generation to follow His pattern in the task of establishing and building His church.

The New Testament Church

One of the things I am asked most often as a minister is, "What kind of church is the Church of Christ?" I serve a congregation of the church of Christ and so people are invariably curious and anxious to figure out what "type" or what denomination I and my church fit into. Of course this is normal considering what I have explained about churches in this lesson.

I tell people that the "Church of Christ" is a New Testament church. This means that our goal is to follow the "pattern" for the church contained in the New Testament as carefully as we can so we will resemble that church. This is important because Jesus said, "I will build My church" (Matthew 16:18). In the rest of the New Testament the writers describe what that church did, how it was organized, and how it functioned.

We want to be that church, nothing more and nothing less. Of course, we are not alone in this. There are tens of thousands of other churches around the world striving for the same thing and we are one with them.

Now, here is a disclaimer: have we achieved our goal of becoming that perfect model yet? No! Why?

- We do not understand everything in the scripture yet and we do not always agree with our brothers and sisters on everything.

- And we are sinners, imperfect people who don't always do the things we do understand.

However, here is the motivation and encouragement that keeps us going. We know that this is the right target to shoot for as a church. Using only God's word to produce God's church - this is what a New Testament church does and how it is different.

So when you visit a Church of Christ realize that you are in an assembly that tries to support all of its teachings and practices with the teachings and practices of the church found in the New Testament, no additions, no changes. We believe that this is the only way to accomplish the 3 main goals of the church given to it by Jesus:

1. To reach and save the lost - Matthew 28:18-20

2. To build His church (His way) - Matthew 16:18

3. To create and maintain unity in the church - John 17:11b

If you are not in the church then I encourage you to believe in Jesus, repent of your sins, and be baptized today so the Lord will add you to His glorious church.

#6 - The Bible
Discussion Questions

What one thing would you change in order for your church to become more like the church in the Bible? How would you do it?

Is unity among all Christians actually possible? Why hasn't it happened?

What is the most common misconception of Christ and how can it be changed?

7.
THE CHRISTIAN LIFESTYLE

In this book we have covered some of the basic ideas and teachings of Christianity. In our final chapter I want to give you a description of what the Christian lifestyle is like and hopefully dispel some false images of Christianity that many hold to.

Misconceptions About the Christian Lifestyle

I suppose that the two most popular misconceptions about the Christian lifestyle are:

1. You are not allowed to do anything that is "fun."

In other words, when you become a Christian you have to abandon most of the things that you enjoyed doing before you became a Christian. The idea is that Christianity is about obeying a strict set of rules.

2. All you do as a Christian is go to church.

Many people refuse to become Christians because they are afraid that they will be obliged to attend church all the time. The false idea that Christianity is mostly about attending worship services once, twice, even three times per week.

There is a germ of truth to these two ideas, but in the end they are expressed in such a way that distorts the true lifestyle experienced by one who becomes a Christian.

The True Christian Lifestyle

When someone becomes a Christian they should expect a change in their lifestyle for several reasons:

1. They have come under a new circle of influence.

Paul explains this in the epistle to the Colossians.

> For He rescued us from the domain of darkness,
> and transferred us to the kingdom of His beloved
> Son,
> - Colossians 1:13

In this Paul compares the ideas, philosophies, and motivations of the material world to the teachings, revelations, and leadership of Christ.

One, he says, is darkness and the other is light. Since Christians now live by a different set of realities and values there is bound to be a change in thinking and behavior. Now the words of Christ in the Bible, the encouragement of the church and the influence of the Spirit are primary.

2. Christians are motivated by the Holy Spirit of God, not self-motivated.

Before becoming Christians most people are focused on self, or what is important to oneself. Our society is filled with all kinds of programs, books, and experts who promise to help us find or improve ourselves. Governments, movie stars, scientists, authors and every kind of expert want to show us how to be:

- More healthy
- More beautiful
- More secure financially
- More successful
- Better parents
- Better athletes
- Better than our neighbor
- Better for the environment

The focus is always on how to maximize our lives here on earth. How do we make the 70-90 years we have to live the very best. Of course the idea underlying all of this self-motivated improvement is that this life is all there is, so you should make the most of it.

Christians, however, are not motivated by self, not centered on self, not focused on this world exclusively. Jesus said,

> If you were of the world, the world would love its own; but because you are not of the world, but I chose you out of the world, because of this the world hates you.
> - John 15:19

Christians live in this material world and are subject to all of the same challenges, opportunities, and experiences common to everyone except:

- Their motivation is spiritual
- Their goals are spiritual
- Their values are Biblical
- Their focus is life after this life on earth is over

Their object of worship is not self or the things important to self, but rather Jesus Christ, the one who offers eternal life.

This difference in life-center, difference in life objectives, is what creates the unique Christian lifestyle. It is a lifestyle not marked out by a change in clothing. There is no uniform or special dress needed to be a Christian.

What a Christian puts on is Christ Himself.

Paul said it this way in Galatians 3,

> [26] For you are all sons of God through faith in Christ Jesus. [27] For all of you who were baptized into Christ have clothed yourselves with Christ.
> - Galatians 3:26-27

The Christian lifestyle is the character of Christ being developed and perfected in the character of the Christian on a daily basis. As I said, Christians are subject to all the same experiences as non-Christians, but the difference is that Christians view and react to these as Christ would, not simply as a human being would. For this reason all the elements of life are seen through the vision of Christ, not man. For example:

- The environment is not just for saving, it is for managing and witnessing to God's creative power.

- Money and power are not for hoarding or for fulfilling of self-interest, but for use to the benefit of those in need.

- Conflicts are not resolved through power, but through prayer and forgiveness.

- Stress and worry are replaced with concern and focused prayer.

- Poverty and illness are not simply a curse to be avoided, but an opportunity for service and generosity.

- Trials and obstacles not simply to be overcome, but God's way of testing our faith and creating patience and hope in us.

- Failure and sinfulness are not causes for criticism and shame, but the opportunity to know God's love and forgiveness.

- Finally, death is not to be feared and avoided at all costs, but for the Christians, expected with the courage and confidence of one who will continue to live after death.

These are some of the attitudes and approaches to life experienced by Christians. These attitudes, these goals, this motivation creates a daily lifestyle that is much different than those who have not believed and devoted their lives to Jesus Christ. You may not be able to detect who is a Christian simply by the way he/she dresses (because there is no special dress code or special mark on the outside).

You can, however, discover who are the Christians by the way they live, how they treat other people, and how they deal with this life here on earth. When you observe or live the Christian lifestyle, you will see Christ Himself living and acting in that person's life.

So let us review, I said that there is a change in lifestyle when one becomes a Christian because:

1. He comes into a new circle of influence.

2. He has new or different motivation.

3. Christians' lives have a new direction.

The main activity of most people in the world without Christ is to consume. We consume food, entertainment, money, power, information. We desire to be served, to be praised, to be cared for when we are sick. The Christian lifestyle requires the exact opposite for the follower of Jesus: to empty oneself.

Paul explains it this way in Romans 12,

> [1] Therefore I urge you, brethren, by the mercies of God, to present your bodies a living and holy sacrifice, acceptable to God, which is your spiritual service of worship. [2] And do not be conformed to this world, but be transformed by the renewing of your mind, so that you may prove what the will of God is, that which is good and acceptable and perfect.
> - Romans 12:1-2

As Christ was in service to us, even to the point of offering His life as a payment for our sins, Paul says that our own lives should be spent (or offered as he says) in service to others in the name of Christ. The two main misconceptions about Christian lifestyle:

1. That it is all about rules and removing the joy from life.

2. And that it is mainly exercised by attendance at religious services.

These two ideas are clarified here.

1. True joy comes from knowing and doing God's will. Knowing His will, Paul says, is good and pleasing and perfect for us. He explains that reaching this goal requires Christians not to copy the sinful/evil practices of the world which go against God's will and purpose for our lives. God wants us to have joy, and true pleasure and goodness in life and these come by obeying Him, not from disobeying Him. So when a Christian avoids immoral behavior of any kind; makes an effort to be just, or forgiving, or generous, he is trying to do God's will and know the joy that comes from doing it.

I have never seen much happiness come from adultery, or violence, or dishonesty, or selfishness, or pride, etc. Christianity does not forbid anything that can increase one's peace, joy, and life fulfillment. What God forbids Christians are those actions and attitudes that will take away what is good and perfect in his life. So the Christian lifestyle reflects the manner in which God directs our lives through the teachings of Jesus for our ultimate happiness and eternal life.

The other idea that Christianity is best expressed by going to church is also clarified by Paul in this Bible verse.

2. Paul explains that the truest form of worship is the Christian lifestyle. That Christians offer themselves to God in service. That Christians purify themselves from sinfulness. This is the purest form of worship and very pleasing to God. This does not mean that public worship is not important - it is! But public worship is a time when Christians come together to:

- Praise and worship God publicly.

- Receive instruction and encouragement from their leaders.

- Provide financial support for the work of the church.

- Make a public witness of their faith in Jesus by sharing the communion.

But all of these public actions are based on the fact that each Christian in the church has a Christian lifestyle throughout the week. Otherwise it is simply public hypocrisy.

Christianity is about following Jesus Christ every day.

This exercise is the source of our strength and provides all the rewards of joy, peace, and life eternal. Going to church is where and when Christians come together to share that common strength, joy, peace, and hope for eternal life. If a person is not living the Christian lifestyle during the week, going to church (no matter how many times) will not do him much good. But for the one who is truly following the Lord, church services are a great joy and blessing, not a burden.

I hope this chapter has given you some insights into the Christian lifestyle and will help you in your daily walk with the Lord, whether you are just beginning or have been with Him for many years.

This is the last chapter in this book and I thank you for your interest and participation - God bless you.

#7 - The Christian Lifestyle
Discussion Questions

What is the most common misunderstanding that non-Christians have about you personally as a Christian? How do you respond to this?

How has your Christian walk changed since your baptism to the present day?

If you were to leave a spiritual gift to your great-grandchildren, what would that be? How would it benefit them?

BibleTalk.tv is an Internet Mission Work.

We provide textual Bible teaching material on our website and mobile apps for free. We enable churches and individuals all over the world to have access to high quality Bible materials for personal growth, group study or for teaching in their classes.

The goal of this mission work is to spread the gospel to the greatest number of people using the latest technology available. For the first time in history it is becoming possible to preach the gospel to the entire world at once. BibleTalk.tv is an effort to preach the gospel to all nations every day until Jesus returns.

The Choctaw Church of Christ in Oklahoma City is the sponsoring congregation for this work and provides the oversight for the BibleTalk ministry team. If you would like information on how you can support this ministry, please go to the link provided below.

bibletalk.tv/support

Made in the USA
Middletown, DE
06 December 2019